Plucking A "Poetic" String

"Living and Loving"

A Compilation of Poems and Other Writings

Ora Lee Plummer

Legacy I

To order additional copies of this book, contact:
Xlibris
1-888-795-4274
www.Xlibris.com
Orders@Xlibris.com
729533

THOUGHTS ABOUT POETRY

"Poetry reveals to us the loveliness of nature,
brings back the freshness of youthful feeling,
revives the relish of simple pleasures,
keeps unquenched the enthusiasm
which warmed the springtime of our being,
refines youthful love,
strengthens our interest in human nature,
by vivid delineation of its tenderest
and softest feelings,
and, through the brightness of
its prophetic visions,
helps faith to lay hold on the future life."

—William E. Channing

****

"The office of poetry is not to make us
think accurately, but feel truly."

— Frederick W. Robertson

****

"Poetry is the music of thought,
conveyed to us in the music of language."

— Paul Chatfield

****

"Poetry has been to me its own exceeding great reward: it has given me the habit of wishing to discover the good and beautiful in all that meets and surrounds me."

— Samuel T. Coleridge

ACKNOWLEDGEMENTS

At this point in my life, it is very difficult for me to reach back into the recesses of my mind and try to remember all the people and experiences that helped me to be where I am today, birthing my first book as Legacy I - <u>Plucking A "Poetic" String: "Living and Loving."</u> There are not adequate words to express my HEARTFELT GRATITUDE to everyone, but I WILL DO MY BEST and ask your FORGIVENESS in advance if, for any reason, you feel overlooked or left out, which has not been my intention at all.

- First, I know and will tell YOU that what you will read came totally from GOD who had me write my first poem in 1977 and has given me over fifty poems (with some other writings) through the years. They have been compiled for your reading. I am blessed because He has blessed me, and now I hope you will enjoy some of the overflow...

- Then, I am blessed to be in a "unique biological" family, living in close proximity to most of my siblings; however, some of them may NOT know what I do when I seek refuge in my private space - I THINK AND WRITE, and many of them have little or no clue what I have been writing all these years. My parents and two deceased brothers will not see the final fruit; however, I remember reading some of the poems to my brother Sam when I returned from Paris in 1984. I am very thankful to have had them in my life as long as I did...loving, supporting, and encouraging me in their own individual way - however and whenever...

- *Today, my brother Joseph (with his wife Renee) and my three sisters: Ruth (with her husband Leemon), Joyce, Irma, and Ellene W. Plummer (Sam's widow) are so dear to me. I am very thankful to see another generation – two nieces (Angela and Trina) and nine nephews (Troy, Byron, Chris, Marcus, Isaac, John David, Jason, Sean, and Justin) all moving forward with their spouses and children); in addition, two uncles, two aunts, and many extended family members here and there...too numerous to name. All of you are blessings in my life...*

- *God has blessed me with a truly extraordinary "spiritual" family – Bethany Church in Baton Rouge – where I have been worshipping since 1984 and loving it. The ministry meets the needs of the young and old under the present leadership of Pastor Jonathan Stockstill (who received his lead role from emeritus pastors Roy Stockstill (grandfather) and Larry Stockstill (father). I have Pastor Jonathan's support and enjoy his weekly ministry, along with the other pastors, staff, and leaders. Shirley Moland is just one of many "B" Group leaders who is teaching me and others like Manuella Ragas "to be after God's heart"...*

- *I thank God for my friends (near and far) who have always been a blessing – encouraging and supporting me (Lillie Thompson, Evelyn Albert, Robbia Kelly, Leila Taylor, Marvel Hughes, Daisy Latimer, Florence Wellons, Patricia Brown, Kimberly Michelle Anderson, Dr. Kirstin Squint, my longtime friends in France: John/Christine Webb, Francois/Catherine Boe, Luc/Jocelyn Gourand; as well as Debra Borskey, Orine White, Earnest/ Cherlyn Fitzhugh, Dianne Haydel-Lewis,*

Patricia Hoyt, Joan Rougon and many others I do not have the space to name.

- Then, on October 25, 2015, I met Etta Alexander and we became "kindred spirits as writers" because she loved to "put pen to paper" and so did I! Now we are on an adventure together as writers/poets. And it has blossomed into books for both of us with Xlibris Publishers because of Pastor DeShannon L. Quiett-Wilmer and Marguerite Patrice Payne. The books are being customized by Xlibris Publishing team (Kevin Raymonds, Charles Freemont, Dawn Gibson, Amy Scott and others). Just three days before the production deadline, Mercedese Broussard reviewed this content and offered some useful suggestions.

- Again, my sincere gratitude to YOU ALL (named and unnamed) who have always been here for me, both through your words and by your actions. THE BEST IS YET TO COME!!

IN MEMORIAM

HEARTFELT GRATITUDE AND APPRECIATION
FOR THE LEGACY FROM MY PARENTS

David (1915-1986) and Corean Johnson Plummer (1918-2011)
who encouraged and equipped their seven children
to become productive citizens
in the world marketplace

and

IN REMEMBRANCE OF MY BROTHERS

David Plummer, Jr. (1941-1977)
and Samuel Paul Plummer (1946-1995)
sudden departure from their earthly
existence into eternity at young age

All four of them gave their best...
And God can and will take care of the rest.

To God be the glory for what has
been, is, and will be
according to His timing!

****

"Memory is the treasure-house of the mind
wherein the monuments thereof are kept
and preserved."

— Thomas Fuller

****

PLUCKING A "POETIC" STRING

"LIVING AND LOVING"

DEDICATION

TO YOU ... especially YOU, my beloved family,
Friends, acquaintances, and every reader
For all the blessings
That come with the territory.

What would I have become
And where would I be without YOU ALL
Being so much a part of my life?

YOU have truly helped me to discover, understand,
And appreciate so many secrets
About this ever-changing process
of living and loving.

To my brother and three sisters
Who continue to inspire me in so many ways.
YOU and YOURS have become
My "Raison d'Etre" [REASON TO BE].

Because YOU always strive to
succeed and diligently work
At what YOU know best,
May this collection of poems and
other writings become
A reminder to YOU and YOURS
That I desire to leave a LEGACY
For the next generation!

PLUCKING A "POETIC" STRING

"LIVING AND LOVING"

TABLE OF CONTENTS

PART I

*Introductory Background
and POEMS About Writing*

POEMS

Only Me

How and Why

Thoughts and Feelings

Writing

So Little About So Much

What If...I Can

Maybe...One Day

PLUCKING A "POETIC" STRING

"LIVING AND LOVING"

INTRODUCTION

As far back as I can remember, I have always written about my experiences in places where I met so many interesting people who impacted my thinking and feelings about this ever-changing process of living and loving. I know that many of my thoughts and feelings could and would have been lost forever had I NOT captured them - often poetically - by writing whatever or whenever - sometimes just to pass the time. A lot has happened since I began this writing journey; however, I would not take anything for the transforming power to live and love.

This compilation, entitled <u>Plucking A "Poetic" String</u>: <u>"Living and Loving"</u> (with some others writings) will provide a partial glimpse of just who I am, where I have been, and what I have seen and felt. In the following pages of poems and other writings are some of my MAJOR INSPIRATIONS ALONG THE WAY (starting as far back as 1977). Every encounter with people, places, and things everywhere has taught me a lot about LIFE, and the writings have become a reflection of my experiences.

All the poems and some other selected writings make up this 2015 Legacy I, particularly dedicated to my family, but also shared with close friends, some acquaintances, and others I am meeting every day. May YOU find some thoughts on these pages that will be meaningful enough to remind you of someone you have known or know and *something you have seen or experienced in life that is just too special to forget.*

8 November 2015

THOUGHTS ABOUT WRITING AND THE WRITER

"The writer does the most
who gives his reader the most knowledge,
and takes from him the least time."

— Sidney Smith

"Writing is like religion. Every man
who feels the call must
work out his own salvation."

— George Horace Lorimer

"A writer is dear and necessary for us only
in the measure in which he reveals to
us the inner working of his soul."

— Leo Tolstoi

ONLY ME!

No one will ever write the way I do,
Or think the way I think,
Or feel the way I feel.
For there is and will always be
ONLY ME!

From the beginning of time
God fashioned - ONLY ME.
To live at this time and occupy this space
To be...the ONLY ME,
To think and feel and write the way I do...
ONLY ME!

FRANCE (Paris), July 1984

HOW AND WHY?

How and why did these poetic feelings begin?
I do not know.

Where will they take me?
I do not know.

Nevertheless I have to capture
My inner thoughts and feelings
However and whenever, so often poetically.

For these thoughts and feelings will be lost
In a time and a space
When it is so easy to miss the present,
Being caught in the past
And unable to embrace the future!

FRANCE (Paris), July 1984

THOUGHTS AND FEELINGS

Thoughts, I think...
Remembering the moments
Too special to forget
Hidden within the chambers of my mind.

Feelings, I write about...
Capturing the times
Too precious to forget
Hidden within the chambers of my mind.

FRANCE (Paris), July 1984

WRITING

Writing has always been the only way
I can give reality to my thoughts.
For thoughts are passing, fleeting in space
Slipping away in time
Often and sometimes never to return.

Gone would be much of what I have known
And felt about the times and people
And places I knew long ago.
Only to disappear or be forgotten for all times
In an age where it is so easy to forget!

How often I try to convey what I feel and know,
Only to find words seemingly inadequate
To say what there is within me.

I do not write to be rich or famous
Yet I know that one day I will become
Richer in my mind and spirit
Only because I feel and think
And write the way I do.

A lot of my thoughts and feelings
About the people and places and experiences
I knew so well would have been lost
Forever in an age where it is so easy to forget!

FRANCE (Paris), July/August 1984

SO LITTLE ABOUT SO MUCH

Why do I write so little about everything
That I have seen and felt,
And seemingly say so little in a poem or verse?

Why do I even think writing so little
And using a simple poem or verse can be
Far better than all the rest?

Yet a few words in a poem or verse can
Sum up so much about this age
As they capture the times and places.

Do I think that I will become great
Only because I write and say
So little about so much in poems and verses?

Do I think that I can become
Famous or even rich writing
A simple poem or verse
About what I have seen and felt,
Saying so little about so much?

What matters more than fame,
Riches, or even greatness is knowing
That the mind and spirit need to forever soar,
Reaching higher heights and deeper depths,
Saying perhaps enough about everything.

Now maybe someone will know
A lot more than before
About who I am, what I have felt,
And seen along the way!

For I will leave a legacy
Of my thoughts and feelings
In a few words about my living and loving.

FRANCE (Paris), July 1984

WHAT IF...I CAN

What if...I can capture
The essence of living and loving
Using a few words
Like Solomon defined his time
With wisdom, knowledge, and understanding
Beyond his years
And the essence of living during his age?

What if...I can write
A poem or verse that captures a thought
Which says what I feel and what you think
In a few words?

What if...I can change
The way people see the world
By writing in a few words
Something that can be lost for all times?

What if...I can write
A poem or verse in a way
That it has never been written
And at the time it needed to be written?

What if...I can be
Wise and intelligent
With some understanding
about living and loving?

What if...I can capture
Thoughts and feelings
Too precious to forget?

What if...I do not stop and write
About my thoughts and feelings,
Memories and moments
Too special and precious to forget,
Hidden within the chambers of my mind?

Then all my living and loving now
And my thinking and writing about
People, places, and things
Would be lost forever.

FRANCE (Paris), August 1984

MAYBE...ONE DAY

For so long, I have wanted
To write something about my life,
Maybe create a character in a novel,
Clothed with the realities of my existence.

Perhaps one day...MAYBE.

Maybe...one day
I will be widely read or even well known,
And say something
That captures hearts and minds of many.

Maybe...one day
I will express what can be,
Or has been difficult to say.

Maybe...one day
I will be someone to simply explain
The essence of living and loving,
Or even be recognized for my thinking.

Maybe...one day
I will give life to others
By the way I think and write.

And maybe...one day
I will really be able to say and do
What I truly think and feel,

And maybe...one day
You will know me
By the way I express
My thoughts and feelings.

FRANCE (Paris), August 1984

THOUGHTS ABOUT LIFE

"God gives every man the virtue,
temper, understanding, taste
that lifts him into life,
and lets him fall in just the niche
he was ordained to fill.

Remember that life is neither pain
nor pleasure; it is serious business,
to be entered upon with courage,
and a spirit of self-sacrifice."

— Alexis C.H. de Tocqueville

"Life is divided into three terms -
that was, which is, and which will be.
Let us learn from the past to profit the present,
and from the present to live better for the future..."

— William Wordsworth

"There is pleasure enough in this
life to make us wish to live,
and pain enough to reconcile us to
death when we can live no longer.
The most we can get out of life is
its discipline for ourselves,
and its usefulness for others."

— Tryon Edwards

Part II

Miscellaneous POEMS About Living and Loving

Setbacks
Tomorrow
Because of YOU
Strong Again

ALONE

ALONE, I try to capture the moments.
ALONE, I try to find meaning
And make some sense out of what was
And what is, hoping that what will be...
Unexpectedly does NOT find me
ALONE.

ALONE, I write about people, places,
And experiences that helped me
To understand and appreciate
What it really means to be ALONE.

FRANCE (Paris), July 1984

HERE I AM

Here I am, embracing life
Having known and seen
Far more than so many
Who have also lived and loved.

Here I am, remembering yesterday,
Enjoying today and thinking about tomorrow.

Here I am, knowing now I have the rest
Of my life ahead of me
To truly see and love people,
Places, and things around me.

FRANCE (Paris), July/August 1984

AUTOBIOGRAPHICAL SKETCH: A TODAY'S SELFIE

I, being who I am, challenged myself
To create a "poetic self portrait" on this day,
And let the page come out of ME.
Then, it may or may not be the ultimate truth
However, this will be about ME.

So what follows is my simplistic TODAY'S SELFIE
Or AUTOBIOGRAPHICAL SKETCH
About my life of living and loving
WHEN, WHERE, WHY, and HOW!

So now on this day over seven decades "young"
African American, born in Independence, Louisiana,
My education led me to high school
In Baton Rouge, Southern LAB;
Then to Xavier University in New Orleans.

Over the years, I was blessed to attend
Many other institutions
Like Southern Illinois University in Carbondale,
University of Illinois in Urbana,
Institut Catholique in Paris, France,
And eventually back to Louisiana State University
In Baton Rouge where I now reside.

Oh, so many learning experiences
and opportunities I have had
ALONG THE WAY!

Now retired and able to take INVENTORY,
I have more time to think about
And remember the many people, places
And experiences I have had!

So sitting at my computer,
Pondering the past,
Looking toward the future
With great anticipation,
I can choose what I want to write about
Poetically on this page.

Since YOU and I are here together
On this day in 2015,
And this is my great CHANCE
To impact YOU
In a meaningful way,
I want to write carefully
What I think and feel
and WRITE RIGHT!

It is becoming
Increasingly more difficult
Sometimes to know,
What is true for you and me
At any season of life.

Yet life has taught ME
To be truly grateful
For all my experiences
Of living and loving.

However, I am now far wiser
and still vibrant enough
To reach another generation.

So while YOU and I continue
To find our place
In the many STREAMS OF LIFE,
Being CHALLENGED by so many things,
May YOU and I become even more

Productive, fulfilled, and at peace
With SELF and others
Whom we encounter along the way.

1 October 2014

*Inspired by Langston Hughes'
poem: "Theme for English B"

DELIVERANCE

To walk away
NOT wanting to leave.

To be honest
About hidden thoughts and feelings.

To say NO
When certain desires say YES.

To stop
When you want to go.

To put common senses
Where feelings are.

To promise yourself
NOT to look back
Or even think about the past,

But to go forth
Trying not to remember

And only looking toward the future!

FRANCE (Paris), July/August 1984

BEGINNING

Beginning to remember
NOT to forget
To see and feel something
New and different.

Beginning to know how
To be alive and well
Recognizing the realities
Of this world and the next!

Beginning to think
How wonderful it is
To have known
And seen so much.

Beginning to realize
How blessed I am
For all the people
And things in my life.

Beginning to be
More thankful for everything
As all of this becomes
A part of my present and future.

FRANCE (Paris), July/August 1984

FORGETTING

About people
About places
About things

Sometimes it is NOT
So easy to forget

About people
About places
About things;

All of LIFE is wrapped up
In the past and present

That forgetting is NOT
So easy as it is hard!

FRANCE (Paris), August 1984

TO FORGET

Sometimes we try
To forget the BAD
And want to remember
Only the GOOD.

The past and present converge
As we try to forget
The known past
When the present thrusts us
Toward an uncertain future.

Oftentimes to forget,
We try not to remember,
Yet to forget,
We must not remember!

FRANCE (Paris), July/August 1984

LIFE

Searching...searching
Working...working
Believing...believing
Hoping...hoping

Often void of meaning
While seeking answers
And sometimes feeling lost and alone.

So many turns in the road
Never seemingly coming to the bend
That might be the end.

Standing, looking for life's meaning
While searching and working,
Believing and hoping
To find the real "raison d'etre" for living.

Often no end is in sight,
But always a new beginning
To search and work,
To believe and hope for more.

That's LIFE! C'est la vie!

FRANCE (Paris), July/August 1984

LIVING AND LOVING

To live and love,
There is nothing greater,
And there is nothing better
Than living and loving.

Thought I could be happy,
Living without loving,
Only to learn
That living without loving is like
Giving without receiving.
And giving without receiving
Becomes living without loving.

FRANCE (Paris), July/August 1984

SMILED

Smiled when I remembered
What I was trying to forget.

Smiled when the past
Slipped into my thoughts.

Smiled when I realized
That the past cannot be changed.

Smiled again,
For the present is all there is,
And the future is not known or promised.

FRANCE (Paris), July/August 1984

WAITING AND WANDERING AND WONDERING

How hard it is
Waiting for someone
Or something to come
As time passes.

Wandering while waiting
For someone or something to come
As time passes.

Wondering indeed if someone
Or something will come
As time passes.

Mind wandering, heart wondering
Waiting for someone
Or something to come
As time passes.

Will it be long or not at all
Before something or someone comes
As time passes?

Is it foolish or all a mistake
Waiting and wandering and wondering
If or when someone or something will come
As time passes?

FRANCE (Paris), July/August 1984

ON MY MIND

I woke up this morning
With people, places, and things
On my mind

Far-away people, places, and things
On my mind.

And there was nothing
I could do but face the day
With people, places, and things
On my mind.

Looking back, I remembered and thought about
So many people, places and things
On my mind.

FRANCE (Paris), July/August 1984

YOU...ON MY MIND

You are truly one of the people
On my mind
Far away, you are really one of the people
Occupying my mind.

And there is nothing I can do
But face the day with you far away
On my mind.

So looking back and thinking about you
In a place, doing things far away.
In my mind, I can see you and know you
For you are on my mind.

FRANCE (Paris), July/August 1984

THE PAIN OF LEAVING SOMEONE OR SOMETHING

Oh, what bitter-sweet sorrow
The pain of having to leave
Someone or something.

No words are ever adequate or right to say
Seemingly, when parting or leaving
Something or someone.

When or where
Will we ever meet again?
Unknown to us, as we do not know
Nor can we say.

But sometimes, we must part and leave,
Go our separate ways in time
Continue our lives
As before in another place.

Oh, what sweet-bitter sorrow
The pain of parting or leaving
Something or someone
For we do not know if or when
We will ever meet again.

FRANCE (Paris), Summer 1984

SO LONG...GOOD-BYE

So long...good-bye and fare ye well,
As we return to what we know so well.

Will we remember or forget
What we know and feel
Shared and enjoyed now...for tomorrow?

Will we forget or remember
The times when,
The places where,
We once knew what it was
To be alive and well
Unrestrained by time and space,
Or even our cultural differences?

So long, for we know
We must say good-bye.
For now, maybe tomorrow,
Or forever...NEVER!

So long as we bid each other
Farewell and say good-bye for now,
Until time and space and culture
Bid us meet again
Together...never...FOREVER!

FRANCE (Paris), July/August 1984

IF ONLY

If only you knew
What I am thinking.

If only you knew
What I am feeling.

If only you could feel
What I feel.

If only your heart, mind,
And spirit could embrace mine.

Then and only then could we really know
The breadth and depth and height
Of what there is in the world
Of what there is between us.

FRANCE (Paris), June/July 1984

QUESTIONS

Will time separate us,
Or distance?

Or will time and distance mean nothing
But space with no meaning?

Will it only make us
Transcend these realities
To embrace something
Beyond our own power to recognize?

FRANCE (Paris), August 1984

AS ONE

If only you could know
What I think.
If only you could know
What I feel.
If only you could feel
What I feel.

Then I know that our spirits
Would find each other.
For you and I would think and feel
As one

And there would be nothing
That could separate us.

FRANCE (Paris), August 1984

PROCLAMING BLACK PEOPLE EVERYWHERE *

To all black people still singing their songs: their blues and spirituals and their gospels and their rock and their rap and their reggae and their hip hop, now praying to a known God and kneeling humbly to His power;

To black people everywhere still lending their strength to the years to the now years remembering the gone years and the maybe years speaking and teaching and preaching and doctoring and lawyering moving along ever gaining sometimes losing always knowing but sometimes not quite understanding;

To all black people on the continent of Africa and down in the islands of the Caribbean throughout all the lands of the Americas and Europe and Asia and everywhere eating and drinking working and playing walking and sitting in churches and schools and businesses and municipalities;

To all the years black people had to wait then sit stand march run and fight for their rights to become men and women in places where and in time they learned to accept that they were black yet proud and discovered that they cared not whether anybody understood;

To all black people everywhere who survived all the lynchings mob attacks police brutality hatred and who have the courage to live and love and struggle and go on in the midst of crime economics race wars drugs and violence and who now drink from the fountain of freedom and who know what it is to die from pollution hunger natural disasters AIDS [and now Ebola];

To black people living here and there and everywhere
wandering as the fight goes on and wondering
why everyone cannot live on this planet with full
citizenship and respect;

To all black people who continue to endure sometimes
shunned and avoided without cause often set apart
and separated feared and denied and abused and
misused pushed and pulled and forgotten here and
there and everywhere in the world;

To all black people everywhere who have found the way
to turn hatred into love sorrow into joy war into
peace despair into hope fear into courage;

Behold a new day. Behold a new world. Behold the call
for stronger generations to come forth. Behold all
the gems cut from the stones of time. Behold every
banner waving in the sky. Behold every field ripe
for harvest. Behold the LAMB and the resounding
songs proclaiming a new world a new nation a new
race ready to take the reins of destiny full of joy in
the morning and thanksgiving at eventide!

Spring 1993

*Inspired by Margaret Walker's "For My People"

TO BE BLACK...IN A WORLD

Look around
See how it feels
To be black...in a world.

See what it means
To be black...in the world
Set apart and separated
Lost and alone
Void of the true meaning
Of living and loving
Unlike others...perhaps.

Can any man or woman
Ever be all he/she hopes to be
Black...in a world
Separated and set apart
Along and lost
Void of the true meaning
Of loving and living
Like others...perhaps?

Can any girl or boy
Ever feel all she/he hopes to feel
Black...in the world
Set apart and separated
At this time and in a place
Void of the true meaning
Of living and loving
Like some others...perhaps?

Black... in this world
Knows and sees white...Right
Closer to what some call
The purity of light.

What if there was only white,
Then in the world,
There would be nothing
To determine the purity of light.

Yet black...in a world becomes
Void of the true meaning
Of living and loving.

For being black is so often
Set apart and separated
Shunned and avoided
Feared and denied
Abused and misused
Pushed and pulled
Forgotten!

Black is sometimes never
Quite good enough,
But must always be
A little better
And go a little further.

Black may never be considered
Quite right,
Void of the true meaning
Of living and loving
Like so many others...perhaps
Not as white is...Right!

FRANCE (Paris), August 1984

A MAN...The MAN

It is not so difficult, sometimes quite easy
Finding words to describe
The essence of a man...the man.
For he becomes the image in his own right
Of what it is to be the man...a man.

A being - totally physical and spiritual
Embracing a reality, not perfect;
But good in himself and for himself.
Encompassing that image and likeness
Of God Himself who created this man
In His own likeness and image;
Fashioned from the beginning of time,
Only to occupy this space and time with me.

Less physical than spiritual
Though both a part of his being and essence.
He is in his own right
God-fearing and God-loving,
For without God, he knows that he becomes
Less than he could ever hope to be,
For without Him, a man...the man
Is and will be nothing in himself or by himself.

Spiritually tall and strong,
As a man - ever endeavoring to be
For me, a woman - sometimes weak
Naturally in my own right—
The strength and shoulder on which I can lean,
To share the joys and pains of everyday.

Physically strong and tall
Slender in physique,
Denoting a certain control and ability.

Handsome with piercing eyes
Capable of reaching the depth of the soul
And spirit as this is open to him,
For he cares enough to penetrate beyond
What lies on the surface and to reach beneath
And capture all the lost dreams of yesterday.

His spirit is loving and kind, warm and gentle,
For who and how is a man...the man
Who has no love and kindness
No warmth and gentleness?

A loving and kind, warm and gentle man
Will make even the coldest heart come alive,
Sparkle and radiate a glow
That grows brighter by night
And not dimmer by day
That grows brighter and not dimmer
Day by day and night after night.

Within the chambers of this man's mind lie
Wisdom, knowledge, and understanding
About the things of this world and the next.
For how can a man live and love well
If he is not wise and intelligent
About the realities of both worlds?

His total disposition is always
Generous and humorous,
For such a spirit will make any heart merry
When times are hard and days are long.
A merry heart is like a medicine
For the body, mind, and spirit.

Physically, the man...a man is one
Who is strong and tall,
Handsome, yet slender in physique
With piercing, knowing eyes.

But spiritually, above all, a man...the man is
God-loving and God-fearing
Kind and warm and gentle
And humorous and generous.

He is the man...a man,
As God alone has fashioned him
To occupy this time
And share this space with a woman (me).

Seemingly a mere image of someone
Or something perfect
Only good and right, as he is a reality
Created by God, in His likeness
Placed within the realm of my conception
To love and understand and appreciate
For he is the man...a man!

FRANCE (Paris), Summer 1984

THE GENTLE DOVE AND A MIGHTY THORN-BIRD

Sometimes, a gentle dove from the past
Comes alive again in the mind
Making it so difficult for the heart to soar.

Sometimes, this gentle dove from the past
Invades our being
And a mighty thorn-bird is born.
And there is nothing we can do,
As the mind and spirit search to conquer
This mighty thorn-bird of the present
Hoping to recapture the gentle dove
From the past invading our thoughts and feelings

This mighty thorn-bird of the past
Hauntingly reminds us always
Of times when,
Of places where, and
Of people once known so well.

Oftentimes, this mighty thorn-bird
Unlocks thoughts and feelings from the past,
Hidden within the chambers of the mind.

Yet the gentle dove from the past can rekindle
And cause the mind and spirit to soar again;
As the mind and spirit seek to forget the past
And capture something truly real
About this world and the next.

9 January 1985

SEARCHING AND HOPING

Oftentimes, we search and hope
For what we do not know;
Sometimes, we think that there is
Something more.
Oftentimes, we miss the present
Searching and hoping
For what we do not know.

Why do we search and hope
For what we do not know?
Often what we have is probably
Far better than what we think,
Far better than what we realize,
Far better than what we are
Searching and hoping for.

FRANCE (Paris), August 1984

THREE ROSES WITH A KISS AND ALL MY LOVE

So warmly today, I offer you
A rose with a kiss and all my love
To say "thank you" for being who you are
To be remembered today...for tomorrow.

So sweetly today, I give you
Another rose with a kiss and all my love
To say "thank you" for what you gave me
To be remembered...later and forever.

So quietly today, I bring you
A third rose with a kiss and all my love
To say "thank you" for what you taught me
To be remembered now...for always and forever.

So warmly, sweetly, and very quietly today,
I place these three roses before you
With all my love and say again "thank you,"
For having been who you are,
For all you have given me,
And for what you taught me
About living and loving
Along the way.

FRANCE (Paris), July 1984

DEEPLY AND PROFOUNDLY...TO YOU

You are and were the first to know
I could feel and think
Deeply and profoundly.

You were and are the first to make me
Think and feel
Profoundly and deeply.

For that, I dedicate all
My deep feelings and profound thoughts
TO YOU!

FRANCE (Paris), August 1984

IN YOU MUST BE

Companionship
Friendship
Love

Someone to laugh with,
And talk to and share all the pains,
And joys of living and loving.

Someone to spoil and to love,
And to run home to,
And sometimes run away from,
Or out into the first rain or snow fall!

So you are
My companion,
My friend,
And my beloved!

FRANCE (Paris), SUMMER 1984

TWO WORLDS

Two worlds - far apart
Two worlds - different
Two worlds - separated
By time, space, and culture.

Is it possible to transcend
Time, space, and culture?

Only God can make all that matters
Right and good
Where there are two worlds
Far apart and different
Separated by time, space, and culture.

FRANCE (Paris), Summer 1984

PAIN

To know, love, or care about someone
To want to be ever so near
To desire something that is out of sight,
Yet not out of mind.

To be so close, yet so far apart
Knowing that it is more
Or less than it ought to be.

To receive something,
Yet knowing it can never be,
And feeling that it should never be.

Trying to forget the good times
Of sharing and caring;

Trying not to remember
What was,
And what is,
And not knowing what will be.

That's PAIN!

FRANCE (Paris), Summer 1984

HURT

The mind will not stop
As the memories
Of what I know and feel
Return to the moments I had.

And it hurts
A little too often
As I force the memories from my mind
About what I feel and know
Return to the moments I have.

And it still hurts
A little too much
As I push all these memories
From my mind
And return to what I know so well.

FRANCE (Paris), Summer 1984

LESS PAINFUL AND MORE PAINFUL

Knowing and caring for you
Wanting to be with you
Enjoying your presence
Knowing that it is more than it should be.

Reaching out and receiving something
That should never be.

Forgetting the times of sharing,
While remembering the moments of caring;
With each passing day,
Together all of this becomes
Less painful and more painful!

FRANCE (Paris), Summer 1984

BECAUSE OF YOU

I am here
Meeting people
Visiting places,
And seeing some interesting things
Thinking about the past and present,
The future now seems more certain.

Because of YOU
The world now seems more beautiful
Each time I learn something new
And I marvel at the wonders of life.

Because of YOU
Life is becoming more satisfying
Every time I see all the people,
Places, and things around me.

Because of YOU
I do not feel alone now
As I enjoy your presence.
The world seems entirely different
All around me.

Because of YOU
Tomorrow will be another day
Full of joy, hope, and love for YOU.

Because of YOU
The wonders of this life are becoming
More extraordinary.
When I think about my past
The present becomes happier
And more satisfying
When I embrace the future
Because of YOU!

31 January 2012

SETBACKS

Setbacks, not defeats
Come unexpectedly
For no reason against all plans.

No explanation can ease the pain.
Feelings of disappointment
Invade the mind and spirit,
As shame and pride can never hide
This feeling wrapped up in the mind.

Setbacks, not defeats
Often come for a season
No one or nothing can ease
The feelings of pain,
And the shame and pride
That we want to hide.

7 May 1985

TOMORROW

Tomorrow will be today
As today was once tomorrow.
And yesterday was once today and tomorrow.

For tomorrow is today and will be yesterday.
As we are, we will be sometimes as we were.
For today was tomorrow and will be yesterday.

So we are forever living for tomorrow,
But what we should live for is today.
For soon it will be yesterday,
And we will miss today
As it becomes yesterday as we are
Looking for tomorrow.

FRANCE (Paris), Summer 1984

STRONG AGAIN

To be strong again,
It took my mind and spirit.

To be strong again,
It took all my senses and feelings.

Were it not for my mind and senses
My feelings and spirit would not have let me
Be strong again.

To be strong again,
It took following my mind and heeding
my senses; it took guarding my feelings
and NOT forgetting my spirit.

But I am strong again!

FRANCE (Paris), Summer 1984/December 2015

TRAVELLING

THOUGHTS ABOUT TRAVEL AND TRAVELLING

*"Travel gives a character of experience
to our knowledge, and brings the figures
on the tablet of memory into strong relief."*

— Henry Tuckerman

*"The use of travelling is to regulate
imagination by reality, and
instead of thinking how things may be,
to see them as they are."*

— Samuel Johnson

*"The world is a great book, of which they
who never stir from home
read only a page."*

— Saint Augustine

PART III

POEMS About Travelling:
Meeting People, Seeing Places and Things

POEMS

Travelling

Paris...Paris...Paris

If You Could See Me Now

BRUSSELS/BRUXELLES...and Mannequin Pis

Martinique

Much the Same Everywhere

TRAVELLING

Visiting far-away places,
Seeing far-away things, and
Meeting far-away people.

Far-away
People, places, and things.

Oh! How they change
Thoughts and feelings!

Each place - something new and different
Not found anywhere else sometimes
France's Eiffel Tower, Germany's beer
Austria's chalets, Rome's Vatican
Switzerland's Alps, Brussels' Mannequin PIS
All so extraordinarily different
Even from Africa's Palais Royal
And London's Big Ben.

Travelling, seeing and enjoying
The wonderful people, places, and things;
Oh! How this all changes
Thoughts and feelings!

FRANCE (Paris), July/August 1984

PARIS...PARIS...PARIS

Always busy subway stations – the METRO
Sometimes dirty streets
And "Kak-kak" here and there,
Often crowded with people
Who are going and coming
And wanting to see the old and new.

A lot of traffic and so many taxis
being driven insanely!
So many Parisians drinking their wine
And passing the time of day in cafes.
Everywhere you go or turn
Somebody going in
And another coming out
Of shops and boutiques.

No lawns and few gardens
Just concrete and sidewalks
And all the smells everywhere.

Mais c'est la vie...c'est la vie!
Et tout le monde aime Paris.

But this is life...it's life!
And everybody loves Paris.

FRANCE (Paris), July 1984

IF YOU COULD SEE ME NOW

Strolling along paths...old and new
Wandering and wondering
If or when something
Or someone will find me
Lost in my dream world
About today and yesterday,
Thinking about tomorrow.

Enjoying what there is
Thinking about what has been
Wondering what will be.

What memories will be hidden
Within the chambers of my mind?
As I go forth...If you could see me now,
What would you think,
If you could see me now?

Wandering along paths...old and new,
Wondering what life holds,
Even why am I here...even while I am here,
Lost in my reverie
About yesterday, today, and tomorrow.

BELGIUM (Brugges), 4 August 1984

BRUSSELS/BRUXELLES...AND MANNEQUIN PIS

Brussels/Bruxelles seemingly built high above
Looks down on winding streets
Filled with Friteries of waffles and fries.

See the Ole Grande Place
So majestic, with strollers from everywhere,
Walking and looking in shops and boutiques
And what everyone sees is little Mannequin Pis!

Visit the splendid Palais Royal
With all its ornate splendor
Magnificent salles with a 2800 lamp chandelier
Shining and glittering for all to see.

Lace everywhere designed to meet
The most refined taste
And made for those who love such finery.
Numerous churches and cathedrals
Beckon all passers-by to enter
And leave their cares behind.

To every visitor's surprise and dismay here,
All those CHIENS - dogs
Walked and strolled
Leaving behind the droppings
For all to avoid or escape.

Anyway look and marvel at Bruxelles/Brussels
Built high above, proclaiming its splendor,
With friteries, lace, and little Mannequin Pis!

BELGIUM (Bruxelles/Brussels), August 1984

MARTINIQUE

Land of flowers, Martinique of the West Indies
Washed by the clear, blue waters
From the Atlantic Ocean and the Caribbean Sea;
White sandy beaches and black shorelines
From Mont Pele.

All along the hills and high mountains
Big fruit trees grow up to the sky;
Full of coconuts, mangoes, and bananas.
And sugar cane and pineapple fields
Always ripen by the radiant sun;
Incessant rains refresh the foliage.

Cool winds, warm breezes, and light showers
Grow the flowers with colors of red, yellow, and orange
Fill all the hills, mountains, and slopes.
Birds twitter and butterflies split the air all day
But at night, crickets make a lot of noise singing.

Some dark, others olive tanned and light,
The people of Martinique
All together very charming in every way
Warm as a summer's breeze,
Embracing all the splendor of this splendid land
In the middle of the Atlantic Ocean.

The men and women of Martinique enjoy every thing
In this land of flowers and fruits, sun and rain,
Beaches and fields, hills and mountains.
This country...this land is to see and its people to know.

Martinique, beautiful and wonderful.
Is this not the island of GOOD memories
Where people always want to return?

MARTINIQUE (West Indies), July 1993

MUCH THE SAME EVERYWHERE

Sometimes people go away hoping to find
Something new and different;
Only to discover
People, places, and things are
Much the same everywhere.

No matter who,
No matter where, and
No matter what...
People, places, and things are
Much the same everywhere!

Leaving home sometimes
Looking for something new and different;
Only to discover
People, places, and things are
Much the same everywhere!

FRANCE (Paris), August 1984

FAMILY

THOUGHTS ABOUT FAMILY AND FAMILIES

"A happy family is but an earlier heaven."

— Sir John Bowring

"Happy are families where the government
of the parents is the reign of affection,
and obedience of the children
the submission of love."

— Francis Bacon

"As are families, so is society. If well ordered,
well instructed, and well governed, they are
the springs from which go forth
the streams of national greatness and prosperity -
of civil order and public happiness."

— William M. Thayer

PART IV

POEMS About My Family and Other Tributes

POEMS

MY FAMILY

Living and loving
Once were parents - a father and a mother -
With three boys and four girls.

Then, one passed away...leaving behind
Two brothers and four sisters.
All uniquely different, but yet the same
For all were the offsprings
Of loving and struggling parents
A Father and Mother
With three boys and four girls.

Not long ago, the children were young and small
Without many cares or worries,
As parents, father and mother, saw to everything.
Living and loving
As the boys and girls grew to become
Big, strong, and tall.

Then, all the children departed
From what they knew
To go to other places;
Yet, again all at once they found themselves
Returning to the same place
They remembered so well
To find there, their "MAMA" and "DADDY"
Still living and loving as before,
For now two boys and four girls,
Brothers and sisters.
All are quite different in many ways;
However, they are still much alike about some things.
Occupying the same space,
As all spring from the same parents
Father "Daddy" and Mother "Mama"
Living and loving as before.

Now one brother and four sisters remain.
Though still very different,
In attitude and outlook,
All now work at home, in school,
In business and in the community.

Together wanting to be all they can be for each other;
And now growing wiser by far
Because of years and experiences.

All now occupy a place in a space
Close by where the parents once lived
Still living and loving
And doing what each knows best.

More than seventy years, Daddy lived
And Mama saw many little ones
During her more than ninety-two years.
Her eleven grandchildren blessed her,
And she lived to see her family legacy grow.
Now more than sixty,
A lot by any count and today still growing.

Oh what a blessing to live, see,
And enjoy another generation!

What has TIME done to and for this family
Of living and loving and struggling parents
Father and Mother
With three boys and four girls?

Although both parents and two brothers are gone,
Those who now remain are still living and loving,
Being all that they can be,
And growing wiser with each passing day!

7 August 1984 /11 September 2015

TO MY DEAR BROTHER

David Plummer, Jr.

I thought I had the time...But I didn't.

So much I should have asked you;
So many ways I could have helped you;
So many times I should have comforted you.
But I didn't.

So much I should have told you;
So many things I could have done for you;
So many times I should have expressed my love.
But I didn't.

So much I should have shared with you;
So many ways I could have cared about you;
So many times I should have said: "I love you."
But I didn't.

And now it is too late.
I thought I had the time,
But I didn't.

And your sudden departure taught me
Never, never wait!

28 November 1977

To DADDY: AGAINST COMING DEATH

Hold out, hold on
Against coming death
As it quietly searches you out
Seeking to invade your body and mind.

Stand strong
Against coming death
As it beckons you
In the stillness of some day or night

Hold on, hold out
Against coming death
As it forces itself into your mind
And destroys your body.

Hold on, hold out
Against coming death
Stand strong against such odds
As it searches you out
In the stillness of some night or day!

6 March 1986

ABOUT DEATH

Death, ever present,
The silent partner of life
Comes in the stillness
Of some unknown day or night
And invades our being.

Death, ever present,
The conqueror of life
Comes to destroy the body
Often in the quietness
Of some unknown night or day.

Death, ever present,
The destroyer of life comes,
And we do not know
When or where or how.

This ever-present partner,
Conqueror,
And destroyer of life
Can seek us out, find us,
And take us to another place
In the stillness and quietness
Of an unknown day or night.

April 1986

HOW GENTLE, WISE, AND DEVOTED YOU WERE

A POEM ABOUT MY DAD

O king, priest, and prophet
How gentle, wise, and devoted you were.
How you made the world a better place
For me, family, and friends.

How you changed the course of time
Rearranged the stars;
Set into orbit a planet of one and seven
Lives which will never be the same,
For they rotated around you
Like planets around the sun.

Life has meaning because you were
King, priest, and prophet
For me, family, and friends
Gentle, wise, and devoted
During all your days.

And now, O king, priest, and prophet
We now know
How gentle, wise, and devoted you were!

June 1986

TRIBUTE TO A MAN, MY DAD

A man lived, my Dad
King, priest, and prophet of his home
Reigned seventy years, ten months, ten days
Only to die, seemingly, a while ago.

A gentle man, my Dad, kind and true
Loved by his wife, my mother,
Reverenced by his children,
My brothers and sisters.

A diligent man, my Dad, hardworking,
Who knew how to lay a foundation
That his children might have a place,
In a space, close by, and have
What he knew to be the best in life
From him with a meaning!

A devoted man, my Dad, beyond this life
Dedicated to his family and the church
To the end that now ALL might
Live and enjoy the fruit of his love and labor.

A wise man, my Dad,
Intelligent beyond his years
Spoke into reality
Dreams for this life and the next
That might create a better generation.

June 1986

MY BROTHER AND SPECIAL FRIEND, SAM

Those who knew SAM well
Witnessed and marveled at our relationship;
So special and most precious in God's sight;
For He alone allowed the love we shared
Patient and kind,
Tender and sensitive to the very end!

Our forty-nine years were filled
With ups and downs;
SAM was always there for me,
And I was there for him.
The good times were better
For we had each other.

As we walked together,
SAM became the wind beneath my wings.
Truly a great loss, SAM is really missed;
Yet I know God can
And will take away the sorrow,
Wipe the tears from my eyes,
And heal the pain I feel in my heart.

As each morning sun brings another day,
SAM is not here for me;
His physical presence, I no longer enjoy.
Seemingly his death is untimely in the natural
And truly unexpected;
Yet the Sovereign Lord, who gives eternal life
To those who are called according to His purpose,
In the end, God works everything for our good.

Thank you, Lord, for all SAM and I had.

Our earthly walk came to an end
So suddenly September 21ˢᵗ.
But I know that SAM is still watching me
And smiling - knowing that he gave his best
And God can take care of the rest!!

October 1995

A POEM ABOUT MY MOTHER, MAMA

Corean Johnson Plummer

I want to...YES, I have to write this poem
About my mother.
Although words are inadequate to describe
All I think and feel
About the ninety-two years MAMA spent
Living and loving
Those around her all the days of her life.

For MAMA became the epitome of a noble woman,
And a daughter and sister and a wife and mother
And a friend to those around her.

I have to...YES, I want to write this poem
About MAMA
To say for all times how much I love her
For everything she did for me
Through the years, beginning with giving me LIFE,
Then faith and hope
That shaped my being
And the essence of so many others.

I want to...YES, I have to write this poem
About my mother
That tells the world how she lived and loved
And how much I owe her for what she told me
That moved me towards my destiny
In this ever-changing, challenging world
In which I sometimes find myself.

I have to...YES, I want to write this poem
About MAMA.
Most especially now, since I can
No longer enjoy her physical presence,

Her spirit lingers to lead me
To another time and place.
And when my feelings and the memories
about her become less intense
As the days, weeks, months, and years go by,
I will remember her for what she taught me
About living and loving and being
A daughter, sister, wife, mother, and a friend.

And I will always have this poem
As a reminder of MAMA, my mother,
who will be a part of me as long as I live and love
And have my being because her life
Epitomized such strength, determination,
Unwavering faith, and prayer.
And I will be eternally grateful to God
For allowing MAMA to be my mother,
Who knew how to live, love, and impact
So many lives around her.

15 January 2012

A TRIBUTE TO FLORENCE JOHNSON SPEARS

April 6, 1930 – November 19, 2004

Sometimes it is difficult to put into words the feelings we have when a dearly beloved wife, mother, sister, aunt, and friend departs and enters eternal rest. Easing the grief of not having her physical presence that we have enjoyed for so many years is greatly intensified; yet we all must try to have an earthly and eternal perspective as we remember her life and legacy. Florence Johnson Spears' mere presence always brought a "ray of sunshine" into the lives of all who knew her. Yet, so many of us who are left behind believe that she is just away in a place of light and peace where God's eternal love truly abounds.

Her worldly difficulties (if any) have ceased, and now she has gone to her eternal rest. Yet the memories of her living and loving us all still remain in our hearts and minds today...for tomorrow and forever until we all go to the place where our spirits will join hers.

For those of us who remain behind – husband, children, family, friends, and acquaintances, may we come to fully know that her living and loving us was not in vain. As the days become weeks and weeks become months and months become years, may we also sense that the memories we hold in our own private chambers will transcend the feelings only time can heal.

"So let us not grieve too much, shed unnecessary tears, hug our sorrow too long, and feed our loneliness with empty days"...BUT let us go on knowing that our "beloved" Florence gave her best by the life she lived and the love she gave to all of us...and now God can and will take care of the rest!

8 December 2004

PART V

Some Major Writings and Final Poetic Thoughts

Fare Ye Well To Dr. Kirstin Squint

On Your Wedding Day to Kimberly Michelle and Tracey Lamar Anderson

Defining Experiences in Teaching: Continuing to Impact Another Generation

Thinking About Life and the Reality of Dreams

I THANK GOD

THOUGHTS ABOUT THE POET AS ARTIST

"Everything which I have created
as a poet has had its origin
in a frame of mind and a situation in life;
I never wrote because I had, as they say,
found a good subject."

— Henrik Ibsen

"The artist (in literature) appeals to
that part of our being
which is not dependent on wisdom;
to that in us which is a gift
and not an acquisition —
and, therefore, more permanently enduring.
He speaks to our capacity for delight and wonder,
to our sense of mystery surrounding our lives;
to our sense of pity, and beauty, and pain."

— Joseph Conrad

"Poets utter great and wise things
which they do not themselves understand."

— Plato

FARE YE WELL TO DR. KIRSTIN SQUINT

Today, it is with mixed feelings that I stand before you and bid Dr. Squint Fare Ye Well, as the English would say. She is about to leave colleagues and friends of the Department of English after five years of full-time teaching which began in 2005.

Dr. Squint was assigned as my office partner when she came to Southern University. As fellow colleagues, our relationship was one of respect, and I learned about some of her achievements to date: Bachelor of Arts in English from Eureka College in 1995, Master of Arts from Miami University in 1998, and the Ph.D. in Comparative Literature from Louisiana State University in 2008.

Dr. Squint began her teaching career in 1997 as a high school language arts teacher on a Navajo Reservation in New Mexico. Then she spent five years in community colleges (three as a full-time faculty member in Flagstaff, AZ) before coming to Louisiana in 2003 to pursue the Ph.D. (which Dr. Squint admirably completed in 2008). Dr. Squint has presented her research and other interests at numerous conferences and has published in the areas of Native American, Caribbean American, and African American literature. Currently, her book, _Native Spirituality and Literary Resistance_, is under review for publication at the University of New Mexico Press.

From the beginning, Dr. Squint and I had much in common; I recognized her great love for teaching as a profession and craft. Her dedication and concern for student achievement and learning were continuously demonstrated in her interaction with all her students. A very energetic, hardworking, dedicated, devoted *professor, professionally prepared and intelligent, still outstandingly young are all positive qualities Dr. Squint will take to High Point University in North Carolina this fall in her new position as Assistant Professor of English (major focus in multiethnic literature.)*

Dr. Squint will be greatly missed for the qualities she possesses; however, at this farewell gathering of colleagues and friends, we all wish her every success and favor as she writes another career chapter in North Carolina. And I pray that God continues to bless and keep Dr. Kirstin Squint in every area of her life along the way!

May 2010

ON YOUR WEDDING DAY TO KIMBERLY MICHELLE AND TRACEY LAMAR ANDERSON

What a blessing to LOVE and BE LOVED...to believe that you have found it and want to share this love with another human being. It is one of the pivotal moments in life when two people who were once strangers are drawn together by an irresistible attraction, so their souls cannot be separated neither by time nor space nor person nor thing.

When a man sees in a woman that dream of love and sweetness which has haunted his soul, and when in love a woman finds the rest and satisfaction her heart has been seeking, it is a revelation from above, and it comes from the hand of God; this LOVE makes all things new.

ON YOUR WEDDING DAY, you are performing an act of utter faith, believing in one another now and for always. Other blessings will come to you for making the commitment to follow God's ordinances of Holy Matrimony.

I believe that you are indeed happy tonight, and may happiness follow both of you for the rest of your lives as you go forth together into the future.

Having known you, Kimberly, for many years, I have watched God blossom you into a beautiful, kind, understanding, "steady" Christian woman who is now spirit-led, purpose driven, hardworking, committed to doing God's will and walking in His ways.

And now, God is joining you and Tracey Lamar because of your love and commitment to each other and your willingness to honor Him because you esteem him as good for you, a gentle man, kind and loving, a man who will likewise honor you as the "weaker vessel," thus treat you exceptionally well and continue to be strong as a man...but most of all God fearing.

I PRAY ON THIS "FULL OF PROMISE" WEDDING EVENING...

- That you will always remember the qualities that attracted you to each other when you first met and how you felt as your feelings of attraction turned to respect, admiration, and finally love...

- That you will work hard to turn your FEELINGS OF LOVE into constant ACTS OF LOVE so that no one or nothing can separate you from your ONENESS...

- That you always have kind and loving hearts that are quick to ask forgiveness when you are wrong as well as to forgive when the other is wrong...

- That your love will grow to bear all things...to accept the good and the bad...to search, believe and hope for the BEST in every situation and have the perseverance to endure all things for better or worse...

- That you will always place your marriage of oneness in God's loving hand and that your love will increase and overflow beyond anything you can yet imagine (tonight and always)...

In the meantime, be happy; grow together, and enjoy living and loving the life you are beginning...together in Holy Matrimony!

3 October 2009

DEFINING EXPERIENCES IN TEACHING: CONTINUING TO IMPACT ANOTHER GENERATION

When I think about defining experiences during my career as a teacher, I realize that forty plus years have gone by so quickly and every experience seems like only a few yesterdays when I began this awesome journey in 1965 (having graduated a semester early from Xavier University of Louisiana). Yet, the challenges have not lessened the satisfaction I have every day when I walk into a classroom and see those eager and sometimes not so eager students, sitting there with their eyes focused on me (the instructor of the moment). During all these years, I have been truly blessed to impact many college students in many places (Louisiana, Illinois, and California to name a few) and probably to a lesser degree around the world (like France, Africa, and Martinique). What an opportunity teaching has afforded me!

Today, after more than forty years, I still have a zest in my spirit and the zeal is as strong as ever for the teaching profession...one that some are born to do. Being a teacher or having been engaged in the art of teaching has become my "raison d'etre"...my purpose...my calling... my avenue (or way) of teaching another generation. Through the years, I have encountered many intriguing minds and hearts...but none that would make me wish that I had pursued any other career except teaching for such satisfaction.

Very recently, I had the occasion to attend an art activity at Southern University, and to my surprise, a young lady whom I had taught years before at Xavier Preparatory High School in New Orleans came up to me and asked, "Aren't you Ms. Plummer?"...to which I responded, "Yes, I am...and did I teach you?" And she said, "Yes, Ma'am at Xavier Prep." "Wow," I said. At that moment I realized that not only did she recognize me, but she also remembered my name after so many years. We chatted for a few minutes and in the course of the conversation, I told her, "It is 'not ever a time' that I do not meet one or two of my former students." This young lady was one of the first students I taught in 1965...and where has the time gone so quickly?

How unforgettable this teacher-student relationship can become and how unbelievable the number of students whose paths have intertwined with mine over the years! Defining experience number one is that a teacher often becomes one of the first role models that most individuals or students encounter on their road toward intellectual growth and spiritual maturation.

Over the years as a teacher, giving every student the best so he/she can and will be transformed has always been forefront in all my thoughts and actions. This has often consumed most of my attention in all my teaching experiences. College teaching is unique because most instructors have only ONE CHANCE (semester) to make a difference before a student moves on and ends up with another instructor, and my one chance has to be directed toward giving and getting the most from the teaching experience at hand. I am never disenchanted by what a student does not know or has failed to learn. My whole attention is focused on "adding more knowledge to what that student already knows and what has been missed along the way." For that reason, I teach to make a difference in the educational development of each individual student that will be life-changing.

Two questions I can positively answer without hesitation and I submit them as my personal assessment at this point: "Has teaching been difficult?" and "Have my teaching experiences been challenging?" "No, not at all."

Every time I have encountered any student on whatever level, I have been intrigued by the mere fact that I have this opportunity once again to help or change him/her for the better, thus making him/her more prepared and productive for the world marketplace. Defining experience number two is that teaching has afforded me an opportunity to make a difference in the lives of so many students, especially when the experience is taken seriously (which I do).

"Two Q's" (questions) I use to challenge all students I teach (especially when I come in contact with them the first time) are "What can I teach you that you do not already know?" and "What can I teach you that will be challenging and life changing, thus making you a more competent, productive student or citizen in the world marketplace?" Defining experience number three is that yesterday's and today's students need to be challenged to become better prepared and to do more in this ever-changing, ever-growing technological society where all of us live and need to fulfill life's destiny and purpose in the broader scheme of God's creation.

While I meander around, I search deeply into the recesses of my mind and want to be sure that what has made me who I am as a teacher all these years will somehow find its way from my heart to this page. I am forced to admit that this writing experience allows me the opportunity to say to the world that teaching is the noblest profession in which anyone can engage because without a teacher somewhere in the course of a life span, many people would not be doing what they are doing. And I know that you at Townsend Press* will have the opportunity to read about so many varied experiences and challenges that so many other teachers have had and are having.

Highlighting certain defining personal teaching experiences can be useful for self-analysis and the value it can be to others. The mere fact and challenge that maybe I can capture the hearts and minds of many teachers everywhere and impact another generation force me to engage in this writing process. Once I wrote a very short poem which simply stated: Nobody will ever write the way I do, /Or think the way I think, /Or feel the way I feel. /For there is and will always be ONLY ME! / From the beginning of time, /God fashioned - Only Me. /To live at this time and occupy this space, /To be...the Only Me, /To think and feel and write the way I do.../ ONLY ME!

These simple words cause other thoughts to develop and out of this spring came: "What if I can capture the essence of life [whether it is through TEACHING] in a few words, /Like Solomon in the days of old/With wisdom, knowledge and understanding /Beyond his years /Defined and explained time and space /The essence of living [teaching] and loving [it]. What if I can write, /A poem or verse /Capture a thought/ which said much of what you and I feel /Which said much of what you and I think /in a few words. /What if I can change the world /By writing in a few words /All that could be lost for all times. /What if I can say something / That had never been said /Or in a way it had never been said, /At a time it needed to be said. /What if I can be wise and intelligent /With an immense understanding about living and loving. /What if I can...with my words /capture thoughts and feelings /Too precious to forget. / Then my thinking and writing would /Never be in vain, /As I would leave behind /Thoughts and feelings /Too special to forget. /What if I never stopped to capture / the thoughts and feelings, memories and moments [even about TEACHING] /Too special and precious to forget /Hidden within the chambers of my mind. /Then all would be lost forever /And much of my living and loving [TEACHING] would have been for nothing [undefined and unstated]."

This brings me to defining experience number four. Taking the time to write my thoughts about teaching may be a source of inspiration to someone else to choose this noble profession as a career option because teaching or having a caring teacher is probably the best way to become who we are! It is sometimes difficult to come to terms with our own self-realization which comes from disciplined STUDY. It is not always what others think we ought or need to know, but we as individuals need KNOWLEDGE to fulfill our destiny and purpose.

Our destiny or purpose is linked to the Creator of the universe and His master plan (whether we are aware or know it) and to know it, I advocate: "Read, read, read, and read more" which is my simple philosophy for living and having a successful, satisfying existence. I know the value of putting "life-giving" thoughts into the minds and hearts of every student [and sharing such thoughts with whomever we meet along the way]. There is a saying, "Nothing in...nothing out." Daily, I try to impart some valuable knowledge, offering great thoughts and ideas from renowned thinkers and trailblazers. Today's students cannot think about what they do not know. Reading is the key to self-realization. If students do not know who they are and the purpose for which they are created, how can they become another generation with character, competent, and productive in the world marketplace?

Finally, perhaps the most defining experience is when I realized that I wanted to be an instrument to loose intellectual bondages and/or shackles that keep our students or young people from being whole, productive, and capable of leading fulfilling lives. Helping them to have character or building them up from within (intellectually, spiritually, and emotionally) has been my great mission for over forty years and continues today as I endeavor to touch another generation. YES, the zest and zeal to change minds and hearts and to inspire renewed thinking about life, love, and issues remain paramount in my thoughts and actions. Other people's beliefs, values, and actions have also become important in today's world of ongoing change.

Years ago, I read Dr. Ben Carson's book, <u>THINK BIG</u>, which transformed my thinking in a meaningful way. He is the very notable African American neurosurgeon who separated the Binder twins, and since then his life and the acronym that Dr. Carson developed have helped young and old, rich and poor to become better citizens in the world marketplace. The acronym, THINK BIG: T stands for TIME and TALENTS to be used wisely as both are gifts from God; H is for HOPE and HONESTY – hope for the "best" and be honest; I is for INSIGHT which can be gotten from people and good books; N stands for NICE; so be nice to everyone. K is for KNOWLEDGE which is the key to living and success. Then B is for BOOKS which are to be read actively and one important source or way to knowledge. I is for IN-DEPTH learning skills which can and should be developed. Finally, G stands for GOD; it is important to never get too big or overly involved. Make God first and foremost in day-to-day affairs.

- Submitted to the Townsend Press, this essay received an award in June 2006.

THINKING ABOUT LIFE AND
THE REALITY OF DREAMS

Thinking about LIFE today
For some, their dreams have become
A reality full of hope and joy.

I remember so many of my dreams
And I want you to know what I feel
About other people's dreams and reality
In the world today.

The reality of other people's dreams
Around the world is NOT
Always full of joy and hope...

Many of their dreams have become
A reality filled with sadness and despair
With pain and toil and emptiness
Until life changes its course
Or death brings an end to it all!

15 November 2015

I THANK GOD

YES, I thank God for having given me
A mind and spirit through the years
To capture what lies within me,
For in Him and through Him
My heart, mind, and spirit will be forever rich
As I owe it all to Him, who has given me
So much along the way, at a time, in an age
Where so much is lost and forgotten
Never to be captured or known.

I thank God for this mind and spirit
To write about what has been and what is
At a time, in a space, at an age
Where much is forgotten and lost
Never to be known or written.

YES, I thank God for being who I am,
For what I have done, where I have been,
And all that I have learned
About living and loving along the way.

YES, I thank God for giving me
What you have read
And for having a mind and heart
Capable of leaving a LEGACY.

A resounding YES, I THANK GOD
For giving me HOPE and a future
With the belief that the best is yet to come,
And also realize that I have
More years behind me
Than I have ahead of me.

Now all my energy should focus
On living victoriously,
And using all the wisdom, knowledge,
And understanding that I now possess
To love those around me;
Just like God loves me, and
Always thank Him for His peace, love, and joy
And the desire to reach another generation!

10 June 2015

About the Author

Ora Lee Plummer is a retired professor from Southern University (2008), with experience teaching English, French, African American literature, and writing seminar for many years. She has also taught at other institutions (including Xavier Preparatory High School, Bethany Christian School (Baker, LA), Baton Rouge Community College, Southern Illinois University (Carbondale), University of Illinois (Urbana), San Jose State University, Chicago State University, Louisiana State University), and she has experience as a college administrator. She received her education and training at Southern University Laboratory High School, followed by Xavier University (New Orleans), Southern Illinois University (Carbondale), Institut Catholique (Paris), Universite d'Abidjan (Ivory Coast), Stanford University (Palo Alto, CA), University of Illinois (Urbana), Louisiana State University (Baton Rouge), Chicago State University. Published in other poetry collections, she is the writer/author of <u>Writing for Success: A "User Friendly" Manual for Effective Communication</u> (1998). Her travel experiences have taken her to France, Africa, England, Germany, Austria, Switzerland, Italy, Belgium, Senegal, Ivory Coast, Canada (Quebec and Montreal), the Caribbean (Bahamas and Martinique), and Israel (Tel Aviv and Jerusalem). Currently, she continues to pursue her interests as a writer/poet, editor, and adult literacy tutor.

For more information, feel free to contact her via e-mail: olplummer@yahoo.com

About the Graphic Designer

As the graphic designer for Angi Weir Grafix, Angela Hubbard-Weir's technical assistance aided the writer during the entire process of compiling this collection: _Plucking A "Poetic" String_, and she also developed the original design for the cover.

For more information, feel free to contact her via e-mail: angelweir08@gmail.com

Printed in the United States
By Bookmasters